The Minister and the Madness:
Seven Days of Casting

by Natalie McMillan

www.MzNatalie.com

DEDICATION:

To the ones who walk into rooms full of
people... and still feel alone. To those who
cast quietly and show up when no one else
will. To the minister who's ministered while
breaking. And to every weary soul called to
serve while unraveling.

And to You, Lord —
who met me in the midst of madness
and whispered me back to peace.

The Minister and the Madness Seven Days
of Casting

This is a work of creative nonfiction. Names,
dialogues, and events have been faithfully
rendered to reflect real conversations and
spiritual truths. Any resemblance to
fictional characters or unrelated persons is
unintended.

Published by L&R Publishing
Garland, Texas, United States
ISBN: 979-8-9945324-5-4

Printed in the United States of America

Cover design and interior layout by Natalie McMillan

For permissions, inquiries, or ministry use, contact:
l.and.rpublishing@gmail.com

NOTE TO THE READER:

If you're tired, unraveling, grieving, or wrestling within yourself and with God — you're not alone.

This is truth for the soul-tired. And prayerfully, a roadmap toward rest.

I invite you to lay your head on:

"Casting all your care upon Him; for He careth for you." — 1 Peter 5:7

And prop your feet on:

"Cast thy burden upon the Lord, and He shall sustain thee..." — Psalm 55:22

You don't have to carry it all anymore.

Let's walk this out together.

TABLE OF CONTENTS:

Introduction: When the Whisper Woke Me

I heard a whisper:

"You've got seven days to let go, and I'll give you rest."

No need to panic — I recognized the voice. I've been hearing it for over two decades. Tried. Tested. Proven. Definitely God.

But still... that whisper startled me.

My first thought? *"This is it."*
Get the house in order. Seven days. Time's up. I'm checking out.

But my spirit wasn't stirred by that. It wasn't death that woke me — it was the **tone**.

Why was He whispering?

He and I wrestle loud. Our conversations usually echo. He moves furniture when we talk. But this time... He was quiet. Gentle. Surgical.

That was unsettling.

No *"Listen and record,"* which has always been the cue to grab a pen and tune in. Instead, the whisper came laced with layers:

1. There was a **time limit** — so whatever this was, it was urgent.

2. I was carrying **something heavy** — something He was now requiring me to drop.

3. I was so **tired** that my own rest wouldn't do. I needed *His* rest.

And if you've ever experienced the difference, you know — God's rest is a realm, not a nap.
It's when He quiets your mind, soothes your body, calms your spirit, and *mends your heart* — all at once.

It's Matthew 11:28 in real time:

"Are you tired? Worn out? Burned out on religion? Come to me. Get away with me... and you'll recover your life. I'll show you

how to take a real rest."
— The Message

But He didn't say, *"Come right now."*
He said, *"You've got seven days."*

He was alerting me to something — and
whispering while He did it.

And that's how this journey began.

Seven days. One whisper.
A body exhausted. A mind in emotional
chaos. A soul willing.
And a story I had to cast to a God I cannot
see. But I know is always there...

DAY ONE:

When Breathing Is the Only Ministry Left

I am a woman by birth, assignment, and identification—she and her suit me just fine. I came here fully equipped with what I needed to carry life, both physically and spiritually. And though time has taught me that pushing doesn't end in the delivery room, I've learned to thank God for the strength to keep pushing—through fears, through changes, through grown children who still need mothering in ways they don't always recognize.

Now I'm retired. Well, *retired* in that ironic sense where the body slows down just as the battles ramp up—new ones, quiet ones. The kind that don't have job descriptions or pay stubs but still cost everything.

I'm also a minister—an evangelist. I didn't choose that path, not at first. But one day I picked up a spiritual phone I didn't even know I owned, and God was on the other end saying, "You ready?" I stepped into the light then—and now here I am, still stepping.

But nothing prepared me for the whisper.

"You've got seven days to let go, and I'll give you rest."

That morning, I had stretched like I always do. Made my bed because not doing so felt like inviting the madness to crawl back in. I wasn't panicked—because I *knew* the voice. It was the same one that carried me through surgeries, setbacks, and sacred moments I still don't talk about. I trusted it. But I admit, I thought He might be talking about death.

Then Tanya called.

Her name lit up my phone just like it always did—faithful, rhythmic, reliable-but her face didn't. It was the floor, her floor. Tanya was lying in her undergarments while EMTs beat a machine into her chest like it owed them breath. Her daughters were there, screaming. The phone wasn't ringing anymore—*grief* was.

I screamed too, because I had eyes that gathered unfiltered information but gained no understanding. And then one of her girls shouted, "They're saying my mommy is dead."

I screamed because I *knew*... but I still couldn't believe.

We had just talked. The day before. Her voice had been strong, maybe a little tired, but still Tanya. Still fiery. Still here. And now—this? Not possible. Not *Tanya*. She was the comeback queen. A champion of "Oh really? Watch me." They told her she wouldn't walk—so she walked faster. Said she'd slur—she sharpened her tongue instead. They underestimated her every time, and each time, she'd prove them wrong.

So, no... not this time. She's not dead. She can't be.

But then I saw it. Her eyes—barely open. Her body—still. That film in her eyes, the thing EMTs could only clear if they closed her

eyelids, the thing I now call "the *block*."
That's when something ancient in me
howled. Loud and low. Not in my throat—
deeper, like in the marrow of my bones. It
was the sound a sister makes when her soul
splits.

And then the volume of the room exploded!

Shrieking. Wailing. It was loud everywhere
from pain that had no words and would
never find any. Her three daughters, three
bright-burning Gen Z flames born on the
same day, just a year apart, were drowning in
a sound I couldn't fix. Each one of them was
strength and sass, ambition and edge,
business-minded and bold. I knew them
from the stories. I loved them from the heart
of a sister-friend. But *they* had lost their
anchor.

And I had not.

Tanya was my friend. My sister. But not my
Savior. And in that moment, I realized: if *I*
couldn't breathe, I couldn't help them find

air either. And if we were all drowning, someone had to come up for air first.

So I chose oxygen.

I inhaled. Deep. Hard. As if my lungs had deflated and were now waking up from centuries of holding things in. It was me fighting for her girls. It was ministry—the only kind I could offer. I steadied enough to speak. "Give the phone to the paramedic," I told her daughter. But instead, the camera passed to her twin, spinning in pain, pacing the floor. She was wailing, sobbing, shaking, and not breathing.

"You've got to breathe, baby!" I cried. "Right now. I just need you to breathe."

And then she did. Not pretty. Not polished. But powerful. A warrior's breath. And I knew: that was *something*. That was *God*. That was Him showing us—*this is how you make it through madness: one breath at a time.*

Finally, the phone made it to the paramedic. His voice was steady but tired. I asked the hard questions, the unspoken ones: "How long have you been working on her?" "Twenty minutes," he said. My stomach dropped.

They were no longer trying to save her. They were waiting.

Waiting on the captain to deliver news, these girls weren't ready to hear.

She came—tall, solemn, in full uniform and carrying a walkie-talkie that took me back to another era. She wasn't cruel, just straightforward. She didn't rush. But her words landed like bricks: *"There's nothing more we can do."*

One daughter begged, "Take her to the hospital. I'll pay for it."
Oh baby girl. In a world that's taught you money can buy everything... *not this time, sweetheart. Not this time...*

And in that moment, I saw the purpose of casting.

Not sweet. Not easy. Not clean. But it is necessary.

In that moment your lungs forget how to move. Your knees betray you. And the ministry of presence becomes the only thing left.

It's the moment a mother, a minister, a sister, and a friend—all occupy the same body—and all of them fall to their knees at once. The pain will shock you into an involuntary silence. Like being asleep but awake.

But I got up.
Made the bed. Again. Just to keep the madness out.

DAY TWO:

The Gift That Didn't Feel Like One

The emotional dams gave out when the bargaining stopped working.

You could see it in the way they pleaded with their mother's still body — offering prayers, promises, and paychecks to an unmovable captain who had already made the call. *No signs of life.* Just stillness. Just silence. Just grief too heavy for words.

One daughter fell to her knees and kissed Tanya's face. "Get up, Mama... show them what you can do." It was a protest, a prayer, a plea — a daughter calling heaven to reverse its decision. The other twin — holding the phone with me on it — either dropped it or threw it. I don't know which. All I know is my view changed, and suddenly I was closer to my friend than I wanted to be.

Her body was swollen. She was still. And death... death is so *quiet.*

Everything in me wanted to look away. I wasn't supposed to see this. Not like this. But something yanked me back into it, sharp and stern: *"Get yourself together. Tag—you are literally IT."*

Then the baby started crawling.

The two-year-old — her grandson — was inching toward his grandmother's body, unaware that the warmth he knew would never again respond. I screamed instinctively: "Get the baby! Somebody get that baby!" It cracked something deep in me, and I sobbed — not like the minister, not like the mature friend, but like the girls. Like a child who just watched her comfort source vanish.

And I was *it?*

In hindsight, I felt like I failed them. Failed her. Failed myself. Failed *God.* I cried like someone with no hope — the very thing we're warned against in the household of faith. But what we wanted in that moment — for her to rise, breathe, fight again — it just wasn't going to happen. The hope wasn't there. Because God had already signed the departure slip. Tanya had exited this side of Glory.

Then I heard it again: the whisper.

"Get it all out. You cannot rest until you get it all out."

I wanted to scream back. *You told me to write, Lord — and every time I tried yesterday, You said "no."* Three times I sat with my hands to the keys, and three times You stopped me. And now—this?

But then came the answer:

"People with sight see what's in front of them.
People with **vision** see what's behind it, beyond it, and beneath it.
Vision requires eyes, heart, and mind — working together.
And when bitterness, anger, heartbreak or envy blocks any one of those...
You'll only see with your eyes.
I'm gifting you *seven days of vision* so you can finally *rest.*"

It was quiet after that.

A holy kind of silence. But I had questions: *How is this a gift?* Watching my best friend gone. Watching her babies broken. Writing through pain so sharp it cuts my fingers before they hit the keys... This is a gift?

And why seven days? If You had let me finish it all yesterday, I would've had this wrapped by now. Day One was pouring from me. I remembered every detail. Today? It's already slipping. I remember the baby crawling — but not what he was wearing. I remember how fast his mother grabbed him — but not if he cried right away or if the scream caught up with him later.

He didn't understand what "Honey" — that's what the grandkids called her — had become.

No more storytelling. No more "Come here, baby." No more lessons whispered in toddler ears about how to speak up and stand tall. That mantle fell straight onto the daughter's shoulders as she rocked her little boy back and forth, both of them crying, both of them orphaned in a way neither of them expected.

And I was still *there*. Watching it unfold like a movie I couldn't pause.

At some point, a police officer arrived. I don't remember when — I only remember the helplessness. I was 300 miles away. And I had no foresight. None.

If I had, I would've done everything different. I would've driven sooner. Argued less. Hugged longer. Listened harder. Stopped being the teacher and become the student again. We were both fighters — and Lord, did we fight. But never dirty. Never below the belt. We loved each other too much for betrayal.

She knew how to cut me and how to cradle me. And I knew how to do the same.

Some friendships only show the good. Ours showed everything.

I remember when she called, late one night:
"Can you go get my baby?"
Groggy and half-awake, I didn't ask why. Just:
"Which one? Where is she? When? Okay.
Don't worry, I've got her."
That's it. She rested in my movement. It was
our movement.

And I called on her the same way.
"Can you go get my son?"
"Yep. Where's he at? Okay. I'll bring a coat
— it's cold."
I didn't have to ask. Just like she didn't. And
I didn't know until now how much I'd miss
that kind of love. That kind of yes. That kind
of sister.

Writing this... I'm tearing up again. So give
me a second... maybe a few.

[...]

Okay.

That policeman asked a lot of questions. The
girls tried to answer through sobs, but they

just didn't know some of the information. So I gave him what I could. He took my info, just in case. And yes, I understand now — because she passed at home, the police have to come. They have to rule things out. At the time, it felt intrusive. But now? I see compassion. I see the kindness in his posture, the patience in his tone. It was noticeable. It was appreciated.

In hindsight — it didn't feel holy. But it was.

DAY THREE: **The Plan Was in Place... But the Price Still Hurts**

She was ready.

Tanya had prepared for this moment in ways most people never do. One call — that's all her daughters had to make. The funeral home picked her up, handled every detail. There was no chaos, no confusion, no debating over caskets or colors or headstones. She had made the decision long ago: *cremation only.* No extravagance, no unnecessary expense. That was Tanya — always practical, always intentional.

She didn't want her girls burdened. She wanted them *equipped.*

We had talked about death — more times than I can count. Laughed about it sometimes. Imagined ourselves living well into our nineties, waving canes and swapping stories. But as we got older, the conversations changed. And as we grew in faith, they changed again. What once was about caskets and colors became about *release and readiness.*

So when that day in March came... she had already done the work. There was no scrambling. No panic. Just a plan. Just the execution of a love letter she'd written in advance. That was her final push — one last way to mother, even in her absence.

She had a church home. A family of faith that didn't just talk care — they *became* it. They covered her. Covered her girls. Covered us. I saw the hand of God not just in the worship, but in the warm meals, the calls, the quiet presence. That's legacy. That's what she left behind.

And now, it's just Day Three... and I'm tired.

Tired of remembering what I swore I wouldn't forget. Tired of rewinding the reel just to feel close again. Is *this* why God gave me seven days? Did He know that by Day Three, my soul would sag under the weight of the memories? That what once came spilling out would now have to be coaxed gently, like grief through a narrow hallway?

Drudging through the past drains me.

These emotions don't just float — they weigh.
I carry them, cradle them, then set them
down only to lift them again the next
morning. Love. Guilt. Laughter. Regret.
Anger. Wonder. Each one with its own voice,
demanding to be heard before I sleep.

I'll hold it again...
Just not tonight.
I'll carry it again...
Tomorrow.

DAY FOUR:

The Weight of the Whisper

I heard Him again.

This time it jolted me from sleep. Not gently. Not symbolically. Literally. I sat up, heart thudding, and wrote it down before the clarity could fade:

"Reconcile who you are and then you can reconcile what you do.
Identity leads purpose.
Purpose cannot lead identity.
You are not who you are because of what you can do.
You can do what you do because of who you are."

What does this have to do with Tanya?

I thought I was writing to *let go* of my friend. That was the assignment, right? To mourn out loud, to bleed clean. But now He's talking about identity and purpose. And here I am — confused again — wondering if He wants me to look *at* her, or *through* her.

The memories flood without warning...

The day Tanya had her stroke in December 2022 wasn't dramatic — except that I didn't speak to her. That was rare. We were both busy, sure. But her sister noticed she hadn't returned their mother's call. And her mother — God rest her powerful soul — figured Tanya was dodging her after a "strong disagreement."

I'm laughing through tears now, hearing Tanya's voice in my head:
"Girl, ain't nobody got time for all of that."

That line. That drag. That drawl. It meant: fight over, case closed. She was comical like that — even when mad. And she never stayed mad long. I envied that.

I read. I analyze. I break things apart with a scalpel mind and a theologian's heart. But Tanya? She *lived.* She didn't need a book — she *was* the book. She hated reading. She asked me to read. She bought every book I wrote... except the last one. "Girl," she said, "I'll get it when you record it. So I can listen."

It stung, I admit. I wanted her to *need* it like
I needed her to read it. But in hindsight, her
no wasn't rejection. It was reality. She didn't
read. But she showed up. For me. For
people she believed in. With her money.
With her presence. With her love.

Two weeks before she passed, I woke up out
of a dream that felt like a fistfight. And I
heard it — clear as thunder: *"Call Tanya.
Read your book."*

So I did.

Her breathing had changed by then — scarred
lungs from years of damage. But I still
believed. *If not for those lungs, she would've
bounced back. I believed that until the end.*
She answered the FaceTime. No lights on in
her hospital room. Morning shadows on her
face.

"Hey girl," I whispered.

She was inhaling and blowing — slow, steady,
determined. I waited.

Then came her response: *"Hey girrll."*
That stretch. That drag. That Tanya.

"How are you feeling?"

"I'm good, girl."
Same stretch. Same exclamation point.

"You feel like listening?"

"Always."

I told her I wanted to read my book to her.
Her eyes *lit up.* "Definitely."
So I promised: *"I'm going to read it to you every day until it's finished."*

And she nodded. Big smile. Still breathing deep, still pushing through.

As I read, awareness came in waves. I noticed everything — the way her chest rose, the flicker in her eyes. There was urgency in that call. But I didn't know why. I was just following orders. Reading like God said. Loving her while I still could.

And I didn't know I was walking straight into the middle of a testimony.

At the time, it felt like a test.

Would Natalie obey?
Would she push past the madness of thinking it was about her?
Would she let go of the offense? The exhaustion? The expectation?

I wasn't grieving. She was still here. I was reading for God's sake — *literally!* And then the Whisper, again:

"Think. You've got to let go so that I can give you rest."

I snapped, internally. *I am thinking! That's all I've been doing!*

She was still here. I was still loving her. Still showing up.

And then... the wall broke.

Memories came crashing in. Breath snatched. Tears rising.

My father — February 2024.
Two friends — cancer.
Caregiving again — August 2024.
My niece — December 2024.
Tanya — March 2025.

Five blows. One year.

How did I forget that? *How did I forget all of it?*

No — don't answer that.
No wait... do. *Why am I remembering it now?*

"You've got to let go so that I can give you rest..."

But You *only* gave me seven days.

"Daughter, all things work together for the good of those who love Me and are called according to My purpose.
Remember what I told you just this morning.
It will help you in the midst... of all madness."

And that was it.
He didn't say no, so I stopped. My brain
hurts. My heart's soaked. My memory is
loud.

And still I whisper:
"Who is this even for? Who will read this?"

Maybe nobody. Maybe just me. Maybe it was
never for the reader. Maybe it was for the
reconciler — the one with the pen.

Because I'm a minister. And I'm not
supposed to say this. But still, I asked:

"Where was God then?"

DAY FIVE:

The Long-handled Spoon

I meant to write more yesterday. I didn't.
And I felt guilty.

I know the Lord hears everything. Sees everything. Knows everything. And I left the page... *questioning Him.*
The woman.
The mother.
The minister.
The mouthpiece of prophecy... questioned the very One who called her?

Yes, Mz. Natalie. That would be you.

But today... today I'm better. Maybe even bolder. Because I've realized something most ministers won't admit: *anger means I'm still alive.* Feeling something — even if it burns — means I haven't gone numb. Yesterday, I broke open. Today, I exhaled.

When my father died, I was the one who stayed behind the scenes.

I was the one who handled what had to be handled. My sister — the one closest in age —

held the legal power. She worked. I worked
too. But I did the legwork.
I honored his request.
Even when it hurt.
Even when he hadn't always honored me.

Honor, I've come to learn, takes on new
shape in adulthood. It's not obedience
anymore. It's embodiment. It's how you
speak. How you show up. How you
represent the home you came from, even
when it wasn't whole.

My father... he wasn't present. There were
seven of us, born to four women. None of us
got the best of him. One sibling is the same
age as my daughter — and while she looks just
like him, she still feels like a stranger to me.
Not out of hate. Just... disconnect.

His death widened the gap.
Not time.
Tolerance.

And grief didn't show up kindly. It showed up like a wrecking ball with names and numbers and loud opinions.

Everyone was angry. Everyone was overwhelmed. Everyone had feelings. Except me.

Because I'd shut mine down. Turned the valve off.
No more arguing.
No more reaching.
No more encouraging.
I went mute in a room full of screams.

I asked God to take the feelings away. And then in the next breath, begged forgiveness for *having* them. I thought that's what honoring Him meant — don't let your humanity override your calling. Don't let your spirit lose to your soul.

But I was struggling.

Not because I didn't love. But because I was starting not to *like*.

Even the ones I was raised with.
Even the ones I used to call.

People crossed lines — not physically, but
emotionally. Relationally.
They said things meant to cut.
Forgot decency.
Dismissed kindness.
And me?
I kept reaching... until one day, I stopped.

And you know what surprised me? The
peace that came with the silence.
No more stress.
No more "Should I call?"
No more wondering if they'd cross the line
again.

I felt... comfort.
Then I felt guilty for the comfort.

So I prayed. And the Lord and I... we've had
a lot of conversations since.

One of those conversations introduced me to
what I now call **"the long-handled spoon."**

No, it's not selfish.
No, it's not wicked.
It's sacred.

It's the tool He gives His prophets, pastors, and people when He says:

*"Keep serving. But from a distance.
Keep loving. But not at your own expense.
Protect what I placed in you... and feed them with wisdom, not proximity."*

It's not cutting people off.
It's cutting access *down* to match the level of **value** they placed on what you carried.

That spoon is not rejection — it's God's protection.
And I'm not guilty anymore.
I'm grateful.

Because I've learned: in crisis, everyone's the loudest. Everyone's needs scream.
And in those moments — *nobody listens.*

So I stopped talking.

And for thinkers like me, for the ministers who chew and swallow the Word — silence is a dangerous thing. Because our minds don't just absorb… they *forecast*. We don't just see with sight — we see with hindsight, insight, foresight.

And when we're convicted, we repent. We grow.
But how do you engage with people who are *never* wrong?
Never convicted?
Never moved to say, *"I'm sorry" — and mean it?*

I've learned that **forgiveness is part of showing yourself friendly.**
It's what keeps your soul from souring.

Yes, it's hard when what you wanted to offer in intimacy — closeness, time, sacred access — is something they didn't value. That stings.

But that's not your sting to hold forever.

Because when people die, so does emotional structure.
Some families hold tight.
Some push away.
Some fracture into factions — all fighting for control.
But loyalty?
It's rarely to each other. It's to outcome. To agenda. To ego.

The day my father died... I was *factionless.*

I brought him to the hospital.
I cleared my calendar.
I was ready to sit and stay — no matter how long.

Not because he earned it.
But because I chose it.

I honored him in his absence — because *that's who I am.*
Because I was raised to show up.
Because I've chosen much — and that "much" is God.

And now... now I'm walking in **vision**, not
just responsibility.
And I can finally say it aloud:

"It wasn't what I wanted to do."

Let's catch our breath here, Natalie. When
you're ready, we'll open Day Six. You've
walked bravely into the heart of hard places
— and still emerged telling the truth. That's
ministry. That's healing.

That's you.

DAY SIX:

Mercy Going, Mercy Coming

He was dying.

My father — struggling to breathe, blood turning acidic, oxygen dropping fast. He was dying, and one of my siblings *knew*, visited, notified us... and then left for work.

And I was livid.

I didn't want to be here. I didn't want to carry this part. I didn't want to be the one to lift another piece of someone else's passing when I hadn't laid down the last one. Because I was still holding that other grief — the one that snuck into my life wearing her best friend badge and daughter-shaped smile.

She wasn't mine by blood. But spiritually, she *was*. Intentional. Respectful. Loud in laughter, sharp in purpose, always pulling others higher. Then one day — gone. Sudden. Violent. Senseless. The accident took her before I had the chance to protect her.

That same morning, I woke up at 1:30 a.m. for no reason.

The accident happened at 1:05.

By the time the Millennials — her friends — called me, I thought they were playing. They joked a lot. They pulled pranks. So I gave them what I thought was righteous indignation... not realizing I was silencing pain. Missing the assignment. Failing the opportunity to *pastor* people who had seen me as a safe place.

So no. I wasn't going to miss this one.
I showed up for my father.

I answered the questions. Made the decisions. Notified every sibling with a blow-by-blow so nobody could say they didn't know. Nobody came.

And I was disappointed in all of it. In them. In him. In me. And if I'm honest? Even in God.

Why let me see the madness and still be powerless to stop it?
Why give me vision and no volunteers?
Why send me into the battlefield alone?

There were seven of us.
Why was I the only one here?

And if I'm here but don't *want* to be, is that even honorable?

Or does it just feel like God keeps assigning me to the battles *He already knows I will lose?*

My father had a DNR. Do Not Resuscitate. But what they don't tell you is it doesn't just mean no CPR when the heart stops. It means *no interventions at all.* Not even comfort care, because technically, that too prolongs life.

So I sat for hours, listening to him *fight* for air. It's a sound that still visits me.

I called two siblings from the "faction" — the ones who supposedly shared this burden. I cried. Broke. They'd never heard me like that. I was always the one with the Word. The hope. The strength.

But I shattered.

One asked, "Do you want us to come?"

I almost lost it. *Want you to? You should be running here! I broke! I shattered right in your ear — and you still have to ask? He's your father, too. And I'm your sister. Shouldn't that be enough?*

But I said... nothing.
Because people will only do what they're moved to do.
And I refused to beg for backup.

The doctor handed me the phone. Said the hospital would honor whatever decision I made. And all I could say was, *"Please, Lord. Don't put this on my shoulders. Don't make me choose. If it's his time, You come get him... without my signature on the release."*

The moment the "D" left my lips...

My father sat up.
Right arm raised.
Eyes wide.
Reaching. For something. For someone.

And then... limp.
Eyes closed.
Breathing fast — but already gone.

"Somebody help him!"
No movement.
"Somebody tell me what's happening!"

A nurse leaned down.
"Ma'am... he has passed."

"No. He's still breathing, see?"

"No ma'am," she said gently. "That's chain-stoking. It's the machine."

The doctor turned it off.
And the breaths stopped.

He wasn't fighting anymore.

His eyes had glassed over before he closed
them. I asked God why. And He answered:

"Daughter, I have told you: no man can look upon Me and live."

"What you saw was My truth — in real time. You looked into his eyes as his soul was crossing over. And My glory had to be shielded... so you could remain. The block allowed him to leave. And allowed you to live."

Mercy going.
Mercy coming.

But I still wish there was another way to learn.
Another way to understand.

Don't put me smack in the middle of the fire, Lord — just show me the flame and I'll listen.

But He knew.

He knew I would ask the questions others don't.
He knew some can't hear the answers — or won't wait for them.

He knew I was built for the battlefield, even when I didn't believe it myself.

Still... I miss not knowing.
There's freedom in ignorance. There's comfort in *not* having 360 sight.

Some people get cocky from confidence. But for me? The knowing makes me cautious.
It humbles me. It reminds me the blade of truth has two edges — one to comfort, the other to cut.

That kind of vision comes at a cost.

Because the longer I stay on this side of Heaven, the less I crave man's applause. And the more I wrestle to keep my alignment — with His Word, His Will, and yes... His **ways**.

Because even though I know His Word...
And I trust His will...
I still struggle with His ways.

And if I do — does that make me a bad
servant?

DAY SEVEN:

The Garden and the Gift

It was 3:42 a.m.

I crept downstairs, realizing I'd forgotten to put up the food — again. But my mother, at 83, had backed me up once more. The caretaker in me is trained. Seasoned. But some mornings, the daughter in me just... aches. Especially now, with a dementia diagnosis hanging quietly over us. I see things I hadn't seen before. Some of them precious. Some... painful.

And like always, I handle it. Like I was raised to do.

I remembered one moment — pregnant with my first child, my legs swollen, my ankles puffed, and me just *tired*. I wasn't sharing. I was complaining. My mother overheard and said, sharp and matter-of-fact:

"Stop all of that. You will get through this. Better women than you have done it."

It stung.

Better? What made them better? Was my pain somehow less valuable? That moment left a mark I carried for years. But now — hindsight offered something holy.

I'd skipped the first part: *"Stop all of that. You will get through this."*

That was the gift. The lesson. The thread. Not that others were better — but that God was *bigger.* He was reminding me: this is part of the walk. Stop complaining about the sacred assignments that don't feel sacred at all.

And then, I heard it again.

The Whisperer.

"Remember the Garden, child. It's important at this hour."

The Garden?

Again?

Not Eden.

Gethsemane.

Not the Garden of innocence, but the one of agony. The one soaked in *nevertheless.*

Recently, I'd been preparing a teaching about U-turns in life — Paul on the Damascus Road, Jonah in the fish. Easy examples. Their transformations were loud, cinematic, preachable.

But the Garden?

That one never preaches clean.

Studying to show yourself approved isn't about memorizing Scripture for applause. It's about wrestling with God in the dark, when obedience is asking for more than you think you have. It's pacing while He's silent. Kneeling while He stays still. It's reading the Word and hearing nothing — until He suddenly says everything.

In the Garden, I saw Him — **Jesus, the man.** Pacing. Kneeling. Agonizing.

I watched as He walked over to His disciples
— Peter, James, John — found them sleeping.
Swatted one. Nudged the others. He wasn't
just tired. He was *hurt*. The people He
needed were near... but not present. He was
alone.

He knelt again and cried out:

"Why have You forsaken Me?"

And I wondered aloud, "Who was He
talking to?"

Then came the Voice.

"Me, child. He was talking to Me."

I gasped.
"God?"
He chuckled.

*"Yes, daughter. I, your Lord. I laugh — just
like you. You're in My image, remember?"*

Then He asked gently:

"What do you see?"

"I see Jesus. Upset. Frustrated that the people He trusted couldn't stay awake."

He sighed.

"Look deeper."

I honed in.

"Jesus the man never stopped being Jesus the Savior. His identity never changed. And identity leads purpose — not the other way around. In order to defeat death, He had to die — according to My will. But death didn't frighten Him. Separation did."

"Separation?"

"Yes. Sin separates. And Jesus was about to carry the sins of the world. That weight meant disconnection from Me — the only connection He had ever truly known. That's what caused the agony."

Then He brought me back to my own father.

"You watched your father gasp for air. You said it meant he wanted to live. But truly? He just didn't want to let go of what he knew."

And suddenly, it clicked.

"Jesus wanted the same thing..."

"Yes, child. He didn't want to disconnect. He saw My will as betrayal. He said, 'Why have You forsaken Me?' not out of rebellion — but heartbreak. Even the Word wrestled with My way. Just like you."

I was stunned.

"You mean... Jesus tried to change Your mind?"

"He did. And still, He chose: 'Nevertheless.'"

Then the Whisper slowed into something heavier. Holier.

*"Not wanting to do My will doesn't make you a bad servant.
Not obeying Me... is another story."*

"Every time you go at My urging, even when you don't want to, your spirit screams, 'Nevertheless.' That war inside — between pleasing yourself and glorifying Me — it's human. The issues of life will determine which one prevails."

"That's why I brought you to the Garden. To check your issues. Face your hurt. Deal with your anger. Accept your own decisions. Greatness doesn't require many followers — just the approval of One."

I was undone.

"So... You're saying I'm not disqualified by the struggle?"

He answered by returning me to Gethsemane.

"When Jesus prayed, sweat became blood. That intensity? That was casting. He casted His burdens. He casted His anger. His frustrations. His disappointment. His pain. His wants. His way.

He casted so that He could say,
'Nevertheless.'
He could not continue unless He casted."

In that moment, the atmosphere changed.

Warm. Inviting. Light.

And I knew — I'd received a gift.

Not just seven days of remembrance.
Seven days of casting.

And I'm lighter now.
Not perfect.
But whole.

I used to fear my own emotions. Believed
feeling too deeply meant my faith was weak.
But I'm learning...

Casting isn't fixing.
It's not dressing it up and calling it holy.
It's dragging every honest ache to the feet of
God and saying, "Here. I can't carry it
anymore."

And if Jesus — both God and man — *had to cast...*

...why did I think I could carry it all myself?

I finally see it.

I am not forsaken. I am framed.
I am not fractured. I'm *forged.*
And my flaws?
They're not a disqualifier.

They're my *credentials.*

I am a real person. A woman.
A mother. A minister.

And every part of me — even the imperfect ones it seems — were perfect...
for His purpose.

FOR YOUR CONSIDERATION

(References are from the New Living Translation)

<u>2 Corinthians 12:9</u>

Each time he said, "My grace is all you need. My power works best in weakness." So now I am glad to boast about my weaknesses, so that the power of Christ can work through me.

<u>Matthew 11:28-29</u>

Then Jesus said, **"Come** to **me**, all of you who are weary and carry heavy burdens, and I will give you rest. Take my yoke upon you. Let me teach you, because I am humble and gentle at heart, and you will find **rest** for your souls.

<u>Hebrews 4:1-3</u>

4 God's promise of entering his rest still stands, so we ought to tremble with fear that some of you might fail to experience it. [2] For this good news—that God has prepared this rest—has been announced to us just as it was to them. But it did them no good because they didn't share the faith of those who listened to God.[a] [8] For only we who believe can enter his rest. As for the others, God said, "In my anger I took an oath:

'They will never enter my place of rest,'"[b] even though this rest has been ready since he made the world.

Proverbs 19:20-21

[20] Get all the advice and instruction you can,
   so you will be wise the rest of your life.

[21] You can make many plans,
   but the Lord's purpose will prevail.

Psalm 116

[1] I love the Lord because he hears my voice
   and my prayer for mercy.
[2] Because he bends down to listen,
   I will pray as long as I have breath!

Isaiah 30:15

¹⁵This is what the Sovereign Lord,
    the Holy One of Israel, says:
"Only in returning to me
    and resting in me will you be saved.
In quietness and confidence is your strength.
    But you would have none of it.

Isaiah 40:28

Have you never heard? Have you never
understood? The Lord is the everlasting
God, the Creator of all the earth. He never
grows weak or **weary**. No one can measure
the depths of his understanding.

CLOSING WORD

*You finished the seven days. But casting?
That never stops. You'll have new weights.
New whispers. New moments when you
don't want to show up but somehow still do.*

Remember this:

Jesus didn't cast once.

*He cast continuously — even with blood in
His sweat. Even when He knew what the
outcome would be.*

*So you keep casting. And God will keep
catching.*

Let this be your reminder:

*You don't have to hold it all. You just have
to bring it to Him.*

Still casting,

— Natalie

About the Author

Natalie is a minister, mentor, and mouthpiece for the broken-hearted.

She has served for over two decades in ministry, carrying both the Word and the weight — often at the same time. Known for her candid, compassionate voice and her unapologetic obedience to God's whisper, Natalie writes the way she lives boldly, prophetically, and fully surrendered... eventually.

She is a mother, caretaker, and woman of deep faith who has walked with grief, disappointment, and divine assignment — sometimes all at the same time.

The Minister and the Madness: Seven Days of Casting is one of several of her published works — born from confrontation rather than concept. It is the product of a divine whisper, a holy wrestling match, and a servant who

showed up when she didn't know if she still
had anything left to give.

Natalie is committed to telling the truth —
even when it trembles — and helping others
do the same.

Connect with her at www.MzNatalie.com

Acknowledgments

First, to **God** — my foundation, my fire, and the One who still whispers when I forget how to breathe. Thank You for trusting me with the weight of this assignment, even when I questioned the call. Your presence turned madness into ministry. Your rest keeps me standing.

To **my mother** — thank you for backing me up, again and again. Even in your quiet moments, your strength has shaped mine. You taught me to serve with grace, to endure with grit, and to love with backbone.

To my **inner circle** — the ones who were *present*, not just *around.* You didn't let me break alone. Thank you for holding space, sending wordless texts, and reminding me that I was still seen. Your presence whispered louder than applause ever could.

This book carries all of you in its pages. You helped me cast. You help me continue.